Blood Glucose Log Book

(60 Day Testing Diary)

Designed by
AJ Garrett

Blood Glucose Log Book
Copyright © 2013 by AJ Garrett

Printed in USA

Table of
Contents

Log Book

Date/ Mood	Breakfast		Lunch		Dinner		Bedtime
	Before	After	Before	After	Before	After	
Blood Glucose							
Ins./ Meds							

If your Blood Glucose reading is unusually high or low; document your food intake in the spaces provided below. By documenting your food intake; you have a better chance of understanding how certain foods react to your body.

Breakfast	
Lunch	
Dinner	

Date/ Mood	Breakfast		Lunch		Dinner		Bedtime
	Before	After	Before	After	Before	After	
Blood Glucose							
Ins./ Meds							

If your Blood Glucose reading is unusually high or low; document your food intake in the spaces provided below. By documenting your food intake; you have a better chance of understanding how certain foods react to your body.

Breakfast	
Lunch	
Dinner	

Date/ Mood	Breakfast		Lunch		Dinner		Bedtime
	Before	After	Before	After	Before	After	
Blood Glucose							
Ins./ Meds							
If your Blood Glucose reading is unusually high or low; document your food intake in the spaces provided below. By documenting your food intake; you have a better chance of understanding how certain foods react to your body.							
Breakfast							
Lunch							
Dinner							

Date/ Mood	Breakfast		Lunch		Dinner		Bedtime
	Before	After	Before	After	Before	After	
Blood Glucose							
Ins./ Meds							

If your Blood Glucose reading is unusually high or low; document your food intake in the spaces provided below. By documenting your food intake; you have a better chance of understanding how certain foods react to your body.

Breakfast	
Lunch	
Dinner	

Date/ Mood	Breakfast		Lunch		Dinner		Bedtime
	Before	After	Before	After	Before	After	
Blood Glucose							
Ins./ Meds							

If your Blood Glucose reading is unusually high or low; document your food intake in the spaces provided below. By documenting your food intake; you have a better chance of understanding how certain foods react to your body.

Breakfast	
Lunch	
Dinner	

Date/ Mood	Breakfast		Lunch		Dinner		Bedtime
	Before	After	Before	After	Before	After	
Blood Glucose							
Ins./ Meds							

If your Blood Glucose reading is unusually high or low; document your food intake in the spaces provided below. By documenting your food intake; you have a better chance of understanding how certain foods react to your body.

Breakfast	
Lunch	
Dinner	

Date/ Mood	Breakfast		Lunch		Dinner		Bedtime
	Before	After	Before	After	Before	After	
Blood Glucose							
Ins./ Meds							

If your Blood Glucose reading is unusually high or low; document your food intake in the spaces provided below. By documenting your food intake; you have a better chance of understanding how certain foods react to your body.

Breakfast	
Lunch	
Dinner	

Date/ Mood	Breakfast		Lunch		Dinner		Bedtime
	Before	After	Before	After	Before	After	
Blood Glucose							
Ins./ Meds							

If your Blood Glucose reading is unusually high or low; document your food intake in the spaces provided below. By documenting your food intake; you have a better chance of understanding how certain foods react to your body.

Breakfast	
Lunch	
Dinner	

Date/ Mood		Breakfast		Lunch		Dinner		Bedtime
		Before	After	Before	After	Before	After	
	Blood Glucose							
	Ins./ Meds							
	If your Blood Glucose reading is unusually high or low; document your food intake in the spaces provided below. By documenting your food intake; you have a better chance of understanding how certain foods react to your body.							
	Breakfast							
	Lunch							
	Dinner							

Date/ Mood		Breakfast		Lunch		Dinner		Bedtime
		Before	After	Before	After	Before	After	
	Blood Glucose							
	Ins./ Meds							
Breakfast								
Lunch								
Dinner								

If your Blood Glucose reading is unusually high or low; document your food intake in the spaces provided below. By documenting your food intake; you have a better chance of understanding how certain foods react to your body.

Date/ Mood	Breakfast		Lunch		Dinner		Bedtime
	Before	After	Before	After	Before	After	
Blood Glucose							
Ins./ Meds							

If your Blood Glucose reading is unusually high or low; document your food intake in the spaces provided below. By documenting your food intake; you have a better chance of understanding how certain foods react to your body.

Breakfast

Lunch

Dinner

Date/Mood	Breakfast		Lunch		Dinner		Bedtime
	Before	After	Before	After	Before	After	
Blood Glucose							
Ins./ Meds							

If your Blood Glucose reading is unusually high or low; document your food intake in the spaces provided below. By documenting your food intake; you have a better chance of understanding how certain foods react to your body.

Breakfast	
Lunch	
Dinner	

Date/ Mood	Breakfast		Lunch		Dinner		Bedtime
	Before	After	Before	After	Before	After	
Blood Glucose							
Ins./ Meds							

If your Blood Glucose reading is unusually high or low; document your food intake in the spaces provided below. By documenting your food intake; you have a better chance of understanding how certain foods react to your body.

Breakfast	
Lunch	
Dinner	

Date/ Mood	Breakfast		Lunch		Dinner		Bedtime
	Before	After	Before	After	Before	After	
Blood Glucose							
Ins./ Meds							

If your Blood Glucose reading is unusually high or low; document your food intake in the spaces provided below. By documenting your food intake; you have a better chance of understanding how certain foods react to your body.

Breakfast	
Lunch	
Dinner	

Date/ Mood	Breakfast		Lunch		Dinner		Bedtime
	Before	After	Before	After	Before	After	
Blood Glucose							
Ins./ Meds							
If your Blood Glucose reading is unusually high or low; document your food intake in the spaces provided below. By documenting your food intake; you have a better chance of understanding how certain foods react to your body.							
Breakfast							
Lunch							
Dinner							

19

Date/ Mood	Breakfast		Lunch		Dinner		Bedtime
	Before	After	Before	After	Before	After	
Blood Glucose							
Ins./ Meds							

If your Blood Glucose reading is unusually high or low; document your food intake in the spaces provided below. By documenting your food intake; you have a better chance of understanding how certain foods react to your body.

Breakfast	
Lunch	
Dinner	

Date/ Mood	Breakfast		Lunch		Dinner		Bedtime
	Before	After	Before	After	Before	After	
Blood Glucose							
Ins./ Meds							
If your Blood Glucose reading is unusually high or low; document your food intake in the spaces provided below. By documenting your food intake; you have a better chance of understanding how certain foods react to your body.							
Breakfast							
Lunch							
Dinner							

21

Date/Mood	Breakfast		Lunch		Dinner		Bedtime
	Before	After	Before	After	Before	After	
Blood Glucose							
Ins./ Meds							

If your Blood Glucose reading is unusually high or low; document your food intake in the spaces provided below. By documenting your food intake; you have a better chance of understanding how certain foods react to your body.

Breakfast	
Lunch	
Dinner	

Date/ Mood	Breakfast		Lunch		Dinner		Bedtime
	Before	After	Before	After	Before	After	
Blood Glucose							
Ins./ Meds							

If your Blood Glucose reading is unusually high or low; document your food intake in the spaces provided below. By documenting your food intake; you have a better chance of understanding how certain foods react to your body.

Breakfast	
Lunch	
Dinner	

Date/ Mood	Breakfast		Lunch		Dinner		Bedtime
	Before	After	Before	After	Before	After	
Blood Glucose							
Ins./ Meds							

If your Blood Glucose reading is unusually high or low; document your food intake in the spaces provided below. By documenting your food intake; you have a better chance of understanding how certain foods react to your body.

Breakfast	
Lunch	
Dinner	

Date/ Mood	Breakfast		Lunch		Dinner		Bedtime
	Before	After	Before	After	Before	After	
Blood Glucose							
Ins./ Meds							
If your Blood Glucose reading is unusually high or low; document your food intake in the spaces provided below. By documenting your food intake; you have a better chance of understanding how certain foods react to your body.							
Breakfast							
Lunch							
Dinner							

25

Date/ Mood	Breakfast		Lunch		Dinner		Bedtime
	Before	After	Before	After	Before	After	
Blood Glucose							
Ins./ Meds							

If your Blood Glucose reading is unusually high or low; document your food intake in the spaces provided below. By documenting your food intake; you have a better chance of understanding how certain foods react to your body.

Breakfast	
Lunch	
Dinner	

Date/ Mood	Breakfast		Lunch		Dinner		Bedtime
	Before	After	Before	After	Before	After	
Blood Glucose							
Ins./ Meds							

If your Blood Glucose reading is unusually high or low; document your food intake in the spaces provided below. By documenting your food intake; you have a better chance of understanding how certain foods react to your body.

Breakfast	
Lunch	
Dinner	

Date/ Mood	Breakfast		Lunch		Dinner		Bedtime
	Before	After	Before	After	Before	After	
Blood Glucose							
Ins./ Meds							
If your Blood Glucose reading is unusually high or low; document your food intake in the spaces provided below. By documenting your food intake; you have a better chance of understanding how certain foods react to your body.							
Breakfast							
Lunch							
Dinner							

Date/ Mood		Breakfast		Lunch		Dinner		Bedtime
		Before	After	Before	After	Before	After	
	Blood Glucose							
	Ins./ Meds							
If your Blood Glucose reading is unusually high or low; document your food intake in the spaces provided below. By documenting your food intake; you have a better chance of understanding how certain foods react to your body.								
	Breakfast							
	Lunch							
	Dinner							

Date/ Mood	Breakfast		Lunch		Dinner		Bedtime
	Before	After	Before	After	Before	After	
Blood Glucose							
Ins./ Meds							

If your Blood Glucose reading is unusually high or low; document your food intake in the spaces provided below. By documenting your food intake; you have a better chance of understanding how certain foods react to your body.

Breakfast	
Lunch	
Dinner	

Date/Mood	Breakfast		Lunch		Dinner		Bedtime
	Before	After	Before	After	Before	After	
Blood Glucose							
Ins./ Meds							

If your Blood Glucose reading is unusually high or low; document your food intake in the spaces provided below. By documenting your food intake; you have a better chance of understanding how certain foods react to your body.

Breakfast

Lunch

Dinner

Date/ Mood	Breakfast		Lunch		Dinner		Bedtime
	Before	After	Before	After	Before	After	
Blood Glucose							
Ins./ Meds							
If your Blood Glucose reading is unusually high or low; document your food intake in the spaces provided below. By documenting your food intake; you have a better chance of understanding how certain foods react to your body.							
Breakfast							
Lunch							
Dinner							

Date/ Mood	Breakfast		Lunch		Dinner		Bedtime
	Before	After	Before	After	Before	After	
Blood Glucose							
Ins./ Meds							
If your Blood Glucose reading is unusually high or low; document your food intake in the spaces provided below. By documenting your food intake; you have a better chance of understanding how certain foods react to your body.							
Breakfast							
Lunch							
Dinner							

33

Date/ Mood	Breakfast		Lunch		Dinner		Bedtime
	Before	After	Before	After	Before	After	
Blood Glucose							
Ins./ Meds							

If your Blood Glucose reading is unusually high or low; document your food intake in the spaces provided below. By documenting your food intake; you have a better chance of understanding how certain foods react to your body.

Breakfast	
Lunch	
Dinner	

Date/ Mood	Breakfast		Lunch		Dinner		Bedtime
	Before	After	Before	After	Before	After	
Blood Glucose							
Ins./ Meds							
If your Blood Glucose reading is unusually high or low; document your food intake in the spaces provided below. By documenting your food intake; you have a better chance of understanding how certain foods react to your body.							
Breakfast							
Lunch							
Dinner							

Date/Mood	Breakfast		Lunch		Dinner		Bedtime
	Before	After	Before	After	Before	After	
Blood Glucose							
Ins./ Meds							

If your Blood Glucose reading is unusually high or low; document your food intake in the spaces provided below. By documenting your food intake; you have a better chance of understanding how certain foods react to your body.

Breakfast	
Lunch	
Dinner	

Date/ Mood	Breakfast		Lunch		Dinner		Bedtime
	Before	After	Before	After	Before	After	
Blood Glucose							
Ins./ Meds							

If your Blood Glucose reading is unusually high or low; document your food intake in the spaces provided below. By documenting your food intake; you have a better chance of understanding how certain foods react to your body.

Breakfast	
Lunch	
Dinner	

Date/ Mood	Breakfast		Lunch		Dinner		Bedtime
	Before	After	Before	After	Before	After	
Blood Glucose							
Ins./ Meds							

If your Blood Glucose reading is unusually high or low; document your food intake in the spaces provided below. By documenting your food intake; you have a better chance of understanding how certain foods react to your body.

Breakfast	
Lunch	
Dinner	

Date/Mood	Breakfast		Lunch		Dinner		Bedtime
	Before	After	Before	After	Before	After	
Blood Glucose							
Ins./ Meds							

If your Blood Glucose reading is unusually high or low; document your food intake in the spaces provided below. By documenting your food intake; you have a better chance of understanding how certain foods react to your body.

Breakfast	
Lunch	
Dinner	

Date/ Mood	Breakfast		Lunch		Dinner		Bedtime
	Before	After	Before	After	Before	After	
Blood Glucose							
Ins./ Meds							

If your Blood Glucose reading is unusually high or low; document your food intake in the spaces provided below. By documenting your food intake; you have a better chance of understanding how certain foods react to your body.

Breakfast	
Lunch	
Dinner	

Date/ Mood		Breakfast		Lunch		Dinner		Bedtime
		Before	After	Before	After	Before	After	
	Blood Glucose							
	Ins./ Meds							
	If your Blood Glucose reading is unusually high or low; document your food intake in the spaces provided below. By documenting your food intake; you have a better chance of understanding how certain foods react to your body.							
	Breakfast							
	Lunch							
	Dinner							

Date/ Mood	Breakfast		Lunch		Dinner		Bedtime
	Before	After	Before	After	Before	After	
Blood Glucose							
Ins./ Meds							

If your Blood Glucose reading is unusually high or low; document your food intake in the spaces provided below. By documenting your food intake; you have a better chance of understanding how certain foods react to your body.

Breakfast	
Lunch	
Dinner	

Date/ Mood		Breakfast		Lunch		Dinner		Bedtime
		Before	After	Before	After	Before	After	
	Blood Glucose							
	Ins./ Meds							
	If your Blood Glucose reading is unusually high or low; document your food intake in the spaces provided below. By documenting your food intake; you have a better chance of understanding how certain foods react to your body.							
	Breakfast							
	Lunch							
	Dinner							

Date/Mood		Breakfast		Lunch		Dinner		Bedtime
		Before	After	Before	After	Before	After	
	Blood Glucose							
	Ins./ Meds							

If your Blood Glucose reading is unusually high or low; document your food intake in the spaces provided below. By documenting your food intake; you have a better chance of understanding how certain foods react to your body.

Breakfast	
Lunch	
Dinner	

Date/Mood	Breakfast		Lunch		Dinner		Bedtime
	Before	After	Before	After	Before	After	
Blood Glucose							
Ins./ Meds							

If your Blood Glucose reading is unusually high or low; document your food intake in the spaces provided below. By documenting your food intake; you have a better chance of understanding how certain foods react to your body.

Breakfast	
Lunch	
Dinner	

Date/Mood	Breakfast		Lunch		Dinner		Bedtime
	Before	After	Before	After	Before	After	
Blood Glucose							
Ins./Meds							

If your Blood Glucose reading is unusually high or low; document your food intake in the spaces provided below. By documenting your food intake; you have a better chance of understanding how certain foods react to your body.

Breakfast	
Lunch	
Dinner	

Date/ Mood	Breakfast		Lunch		Dinner		Bedtime
	Before	After	Before	After	Before	After	
Blood Glucose							
Ins./ Meds							

If your Blood Glucose reading is unusually high or low; document your food intake in the spaces provided below. By documenting your food intake; you have a better chance of understanding how certain foods react to your body.

Breakfast	
Lunch	
Dinner	

Date/Mood	Breakfast		Lunch		Dinner		Bedtime
	Before	After	Before	After	Before	After	
Blood Glucose							
Ins./ Meds							

If your Blood Glucose reading is unusually high or low; document your food intake in the spaces provided below. By documenting your food intake; you have a better chance of understanding how certain foods react to your body.

Breakfast	
Lunch	
Dinner	

48

Date/Mood	Breakfast		Lunch		Dinner		Bedtime
	Before	After	Before	After	Before	After	
Blood Glucose							
Ins./ Meds							

If your Blood Glucose reading is unusually high or low; document your food intake in the spaces provided below. By documenting your food intake; you have a better chance of understanding how certain foods react to your body.

Breakfast	
Lunch	
Dinner	

Date/Mood	Breakfast		Lunch		Dinner		Bedtime
	Before	After	Before	After	Before	After	
Blood Glucose							
Ins./ Meds							

If your Blood Glucose reading is unusually high or low; document your food intake in the spaces provided below. By documenting your food intake; you have a better chance of understanding how certain foods react to your body.

Breakfast	
Lunch	
Dinner	

Date/ Mood	Breakfast		Lunch		Dinner		Bedtime
	Before	After	Before	After	Before	After	
Blood Glucose							
Ins./ Meds							

If your Blood Glucose reading is unusually high or low; document your food intake in the spaces provided below. By documenting your food intake; you have a better chance of understanding how certain foods react to your body.

Breakfast	
Lunch	
Dinner	

Date/Mood	Breakfast		Lunch		Dinner		Bedtime
	Before	After	Before	After	Before	After	
Blood Glucose							
Ins./ Meds							

If your Blood Glucose reading is unusually high or low; document your food intake in the spaces provided below. By documenting your food intake; you have a better chance of understanding how certain foods react to your body.

Breakfast	
Lunch	
Dinner	

Date/Mood		Breakfast		Lunch		Dinner		Bedtime
		Before	After	Before	After	Before	After	
	Blood Glucose							
	Ins./ Meds							
If your Blood Glucose reading is unusually high or low; document your food intake in the spaces provided below. By documenting your food intake; you have a better chance of understanding how certain foods react to your body.								
Breakfast								
Lunch								
Dinner								

Date/Mood	Breakfast		Lunch		Dinner		Bedtime
	Before	After	Before	After	Before	After	
Blood Glucose							
Ins./ Meds							
If your Blood Glucose reading is unusually high or low; document your food intake in the spaces provided below. By documenting your food intake; you have a better chance of understanding how certain foods react to your body.							
Breakfast							
Lunch							
Dinner							

Date/ Mood	Breakfast		Lunch		Dinner		Bedtime
	Before	After	Before	After	Before	After	
Blood Glucose							
Ins./ Meds							

If your Blood Glucose reading is unusually high or low; document your food intake in the spaces provided below. By documenting your food intake; you have a better chance of understanding how certain foods react to your body.

Breakfast	
Lunch	
Dinner	

21 DAYS LEFT (Time to reorder)

Date/Mood	Breakfast		Lunch		Dinner		Bedtime
	Before	After	Before	After	Before	After	
Blood Glucose							
Ins./ Meds							
If your Blood Glucose reading is unusually high or low; document your food intake in the spaces provided below. By documenting your food intake; you have a better chance of understanding how certain foods react to your body.							
Breakfast							
Lunch							
Dinner							

Date/Mood		Breakfast		Lunch		Dinner		Bedtime
		Before	After	Before	After	Before	After	
	Blood Glucose							
	Ins./Meds							
If your Blood Glucose reading is unusually high or low; document your food intake in the spaces provided below. By documenting your food intake; you have a better chance of understanding how certain foods react to your body.								
Breakfast								
Lunch								
Dinner								

Date/Mood	Breakfast		Lunch		Dinner		Bedtime
	Before	After	Before	After	Before	After	
Blood Glucose							
Ins./ Meds							

If your Blood Glucose reading is unusually high or low; document your food intake in the spaces provided below. By documenting your food intake; you have a better chance of understanding how certain foods react to your body.

Breakfast	
Lunch	
Dinner	

Date/ Mood	Breakfast		Lunch		Dinner		Bedtime
	Before	After	Before	After	Before	After	
Blood Glucose							
Ins./ Meds							

If your Blood Glucose reading is unusually high or low; document your food intake in the spaces provided below. By documenting your food intake; you have a better chance of understanding how certain foods react to your body.

Breakfast	
Lunch	
Dinner	

Date/Mood	Breakfast		Lunch		Dinner		Bedtime
	Before	After	Before	After	Before	After	
Blood Glucose							
Ins./ Meds							

If your Blood Glucose reading is unusually high or low; document your food intake in the spaces provided below. By documenting your food intake; you have a better chance of understanding how certain foods react to your body.

Breakfast	
Lunch	
Dinner	

Date/Mood	Breakfast		Lunch		Dinner		Bedtime
	Before	After	Before	After	Before	After	
Blood Glucose							
Ins./ Meds							

If your Blood Glucose reading is unusually high or low; document your food intake in the spaces provided below. By documenting your food intake; you have a better chance of understanding how certain foods react to your body.

Breakfast	
Lunch	
Dinner	

Date/ Mood	Breakfast		Lunch		Dinner		Bedtime
	Before	After	Before	After	Before	After	
Blood Glucose							
Ins./ Meds							

If your Blood Glucose reading is unusually high or low; document your food intake in the spaces provided below. By documenting your food intake; you have a better chance of understanding how certain foods react to your body.

Breakfast	
Lunch	
Dinner	

14 DAYS LEFT (Time to reorder)

Date/Mood	Breakfast		Lunch		Dinner		Bedtime
	Before	After	Before	After	Before	After	
Blood Glucose							
Ins./Meds							

If your Blood Glucose reading is unusually high or low; document your food intake in the spaces provided below. By documenting your food intake; you have a better chance of understanding how certain foods react to your body.

Breakfast	
Lunch	
Dinner	

Date/Mood	Breakfast		Lunch		Dinner		Bedtime
	Before	After	Before	After	Before	After	
Blood Glucose							
Ins./ Meds							
If your Blood Glucose reading is unusually high or low; document your food intake in the spaces provided below. By documenting your food intake; you have a better chance of understanding how certain foods react to your body.							
Breakfast							
Lunch							
Dinner							

Date/ Mood	Breakfast		Lunch		Dinner		Bedtime
	Before	After	Before	After	Before	After	
Blood Glucose							
Ins./ Meds							

If your Blood Glucose reading is unusually high or low; document your food intake in the spaces provided below. By documenting your food intake; you have a better chance of understanding how certain foods react to your body.

Breakfast	
Lunch	
Dinner	

Date/ Mood	Breakfast		Lunch		Dinner		Bedtime
	Before	After	Before	After	Before	After	
Blood Glucose							
Ins./ Meds							
If your Blood Glucose reading is unusually high or low; document your food intake in the spaces provided below. By documenting your food intake; you have a better chance of understanding how certain foods react to your body.							
Breakfast							
Lunch							
Dinner							

Date/Mood		Breakfast		Lunch		Dinner		Bedtime
		Before	After	Before	After	Before	After	
Blood Glucose								
Ins./ Meds								

If your Blood Glucose reading is unusually high or low; document your food intake in the spaces provided below. By documenting your food intake; you have a better chance of understanding how certain foods react to your body.

Breakfast	
Lunch	
Dinner	

Date/Mood	Breakfast		Lunch		Dinner		Bedtime
	Before	After	Before	After	Before	After	
Blood Glucose							
Ins./ Meds							
If your Blood Glucose reading is unusually high or low; document your food intake in the spaces provided below. By documenting your food intake; you have a better chance of understanding how certain foods react to your body.							
Breakfast							
Lunch							
Dinner							

Date/ Mood	Breakfast		Lunch		Dinner		Bedtime
	Before	After	Before	After	Before	After	
Blood Glucose							
Ins./ Meds							

If your Blood Glucose reading is unusually high or low; document your food intake in the spaces provided below. By documenting your food intake; you have a better chance of understanding how certain foods react to your body.

Breakfast	
Lunch	
Dinner	

Date/ Mood	Breakfast		Lunch		Dinner		Bedtime
	Before	After	Before	After	Before	After	
Blood Glucose							
Ins./ Meds							

If your Blood Glucose reading is unusually high or low; document your food intake in the spaces provided below. By documenting your food intake; you have a better chance of understanding how certain foods react to your body.

Breakfast	
Lunch	
Dinner	

Date/Mood	Breakfast		Lunch		Dinner		Bedtime
	Before	After	Before	After	Before	After	
Blood Glucose							
Ins./ Meds							

If your Blood Glucose reading is unusually high or low; document your food intake in the spaces provided below. By documenting your food intake; you have a better chance of understanding how certain foods react to your body.

Breakfast	
Lunch	
Dinner	

Date/Mood	Breakfast		Lunch		Dinner		Bedtime
	Before	After	Before	After	Before	After	
Blood Glucose							
Ins./ Meds							

If your Blood Glucose reading is unusually high or low; document your food intake in the spaces provided below. By documenting your food intake; you have a better chance of understanding how certain foods react to your body.

Breakfast	
Lunch	
Dinner	

Date/Mood		Breakfast		Lunch		Dinner		Bedtime
		Before	After	Before	After	Before	After	
	Blood Glucose							
	Ins./ Meds							

If your Blood Glucose reading is unusually high or low; document your food intake in the spaces provided below. By documenting your food intake; you have a better chance of understanding how certain foods react to your body.

Breakfast	
Lunch	
Dinner	

Date/Mood	Breakfast		Lunch		Dinner		Bedtime
	Before	After	Before	After	Before	After	
Blood Glucose							
Ins./ Meds							

If your Blood Glucose reading is unusually high or low; document your food intake in the spaces provided below. By documenting your food intake; you have a better chance of understanding how certain foods react to your body.

Breakfast	
Lunch	
Dinner	

Date/Mood	Breakfast		Lunch		Dinner		Bedtime
	Before	After	Before	After	Before	After	
Blood Glucose							
Ins./ Meds							

If your Blood Glucose reading is unusually high or low; document your food intake in the spaces provided below. By documenting your food intake; you have a better chance of understanding how certain foods react to your body.

Breakfast	
Lunch	
Dinner	

Diabetic Definitions To Know

**Diabetes:** A disease in which the body doesn't produce or properly use insulin.

**Insulin:** A hormone, insulin unlocks 'doorways' in cells and allows glucose that comes from sugar, starches, and other foods, to enter the cells and be used as energy. Glucose provides the energy that the body needs to function normally and fuel daily activities.

**Type 1 diabetes:** This type of diabetes is attributed to about five percent to 10 percent of all diabetes patients in the United States and results from the body's failure to produce insulin.

**Type 2 diabetes:** This type of diabetes is attributed to about 90 percent to 95 percent of the all diabetes patients in the United States and results from the body's inability to produce sufficient amounts of insulin and the body's resistance to insulin, which means that the body doesn't use insulin effectively.

**Gestational diabetes:** This type of diabetes accounts for about 135,000 diabetes patients annually in the United States and occurs in approximately four percent of pregnant women. While most women recover from gestational diabetes after they give birth, they have an increased risk of developing Type 2 diabetes in the future.

Diabetes Myths vs. Diabetes Facts

Myth: Diabetes is difficult to control.

Fact: Diabetes isn't a curable disease but it can be controlled when patients properly manage their meals, exercise, and the right medications. With the proper guidance and education, patients can prevent and/or minimize many of the more serious complications.

Myth: Persons with diabetes only have to worry about eating sugar.

Fact: Many people who have diabetes incorrectly believe that properly managing diabetes means only reducing their sugar intake. While management of carbohydrate intake (not just sugar as was once recommended) is a critical part of diabetes management, diabetes affects the entire body. Therefore, proper management needs to include a complete wellness plan that extends beyond basic diet guidelines.

Myth: Diabetes support services and education are expensive.

Fact: Diabetes education services are covered by most health insurance plans with a physician referral and plan approval. Medicare will pay for 10 hours of diabetes education within one year, and two hours per year after the first year, as follow-up to basic education. Patients without insurance also have the option of paying out-of-pocket for diabetes education and support services. Diabetes education classes are usually offered free or for a nominal fee, so check your local newspaper for more information on class locations.

Frequently asked questions (FAQs) about diabetes

What causes diabetes?

While an exact cause has not been identified, diabetes is linked to uncontrollable factors such as genetics, race, age, and controllable environmental factors, such as obesity and lack of exercise.

Does diabetes have a cure?

Diabetes isn't a curable disease but it's manageable. With proper management, many of the serious complications can be prevented or minimized.

Who has diabetes and who's at risk?

According to the American Diabetes Association (ADA), about 17 million people in the United States have diabetes, including 11.1 million diagnosed cases and the 5.9 million undiagnosed cases. Approximately one in every three persons has diabetes but doesn't know.

According to the Florida Department of Health:

More than 900,000 adults in Florida were diagnosed with diabetes as of the year 2000.

Approximately 300,000 to 400,000 adults remain undiagnosed.

More Floridians are diagnosed with diabetes than the total population of each of the following states: Alaska, Delaware, North Dakota, South Dakota, Vermont, and Wyoming (based on 1999 estimated population census data).

Diabetes was the seventh leading cause of death among Floridians from 1997 through 1999.

In Florida, more deaths were due to diabetes than HIV/AIDS from 1997 through 1999.

African Americans, Native Americans, Asian Americans, Hispanics/Latinos and Pacific Islanders are at higher risk of developing Type 2 diabetes.

Persons who are obese and/or those who are inactive have a much higher risk of developing Type 2 diabetes.

Age is also a risk factor. More than 20 percent of the U.S. population ages 65 and older have diabetes.

Diabetes isn't just a disease of the elderly. More and more children are developing Type 2 diabetes, an alarming trend that's being partially blamed on the increasing rate of childhood obesity.

What are the complications of diabetes?

People with diabetes develop heart disease at twice the rate of those without diabetes, and 80 percent of people with diabetes die from heart or blood vessel disease.

People with diabetes are five times more likely to have a stroke.

People with diabetes who have already had a stroke are two to four times more likely to have another stroke.

Of the new cases of blindness in persons age 20 to 74, diabetes is the leading cause.

Each year, diabetes causes 12,000 to 24,000 people to lose their sight.

Forty-three percent of new kidney disease cases are attributed to diabetes, and diabetes is the leading cause of end-stage renal disease.

Diabetes is the most frequent cause of nontraumatic lower limb amputations.

Every year, more than 82,000 people with diabetes have amputations, a fact that's not surprising when you consider that the risk of leg amputation alone is 15 to 40 times greater in persons with diabetes.

What are the benefits of properly managing diabetes?

According to the Florida Department of Health, people who can control their diabetes by maintaining normal or close to normal blood sugar levels lower their risk of complications and gain, on average:

Five extra years of life
Five more years of eyesight
Six years free from kidney disease
Six years free from amputations and nerve damage
Enjoy a better quality of life

Where can I learn more about diabetes?

You can learn more by visiting the following web sites:

American Diabetes Association –
www.diabetes.org

National Institute of Diabetes &
Digestive & Kidney Diseases –
www.niddk.nih.gov

Juvenile Diabetes Research Foundation –
www.jdf.org

Centers for Disease Control and Prevention –
www.cdc.gov

National Institutes of Health - www.nih.gov
American Association of Diabetes Educators -
www.diabeteseducator.org

About the Author

AJ was introduced to the publishing world through his breakthrough novella "A Christmas to Remember" (a love story) in 2009. "Life's Pearl" (a historical fiction) was his second published work. Since then he has taken a hiatus to research and prepare for a genre switch to horror. His first horror work will be published in early 2013.

AJ lives in the small town of St. Martinville, Louisiana (U.S.) with his wife Tiffanie. He is also the proud father of three children; Kaine, Korie, and Kalyb. When he isn't writing, he works in the Maritime Industry as a Navigator presently assigned to the Gulf of Mexico.

AJ also owns Rising Eagle Radio (www.RisingEagleRadio.com); a fully licensed member of the Radio Planet, LLC/ LoudCity Radio Network.

Rising Eagle Radio is dedicated to bringing you the best Mainstream and Independent Artists the music industry has to offer. Their dedicated staff members volunteer their valuable time to promote and market the sounds of today and the yester-years.

AJ is a veteran of the United States Army previously assigned to the Headquarters Intelligence and Security Command (Fort Belvoir, Virginia). After his military service, he further served his country as a Peace Officer; working his way from Patrol Deputy to the rank of Patrol Division Commander (Captain) of the Iberia Parish Sheriff's Department (Louisiana).

Within this capacity, AJ was certified by the Federal Bureau of Investigation as a Firearms Instructor. He also trained Louisiana Peace Officers at the Acadiana Law Enforcement Training Academy (University of Louisiana- Lafayette). A few of the subjects he taught included Tactical Firearms Training, Hand to Hand Defensive Tactics, and Constitutional Law.